Welcome to the _____

Family Vacation Book

Place a photo here!

Trip Start Date: _____

Trip End Date: _____

IT ALL STARTED WITH A PLAN...

For our family vacation, we visited _____

Before we packed, we researched!

To find out about our destination, we...
(circle yes or no)

Read travel guides:	YES NO
Read travel magazines:	YES NO
Looked up our destination on the internet:	YES NO
Looked at a map:	YES NO
Picked out restaurants to try:	YES NO
Talked to a travel agent:	YES NO

009886

Other places that we thought about visiting:_____

_____

Our Family Photo

CONVALIDA

VALIDATION

Mod. 71S/TL.SD/1 (RM)

Lire 17.000   Euro 8,78

BIGLIETTO VALIDO PER UNA CORSA
TICKET VALID FOR ONE TRIP

DA
FROM

ROMA TERMINI

FIUMICINO
AEROPORTO

Paste a picture here!

Our traveling group included
(list names here):

_____   _____

_____   _____

_____   _____

Our true trip planner was_____
He/she really made sure that we were ready to go!

PACKING

The kinds of clothes that we packed: _____

_____

_____

We expected the weather to be: _____

_____

_____

The weather was actually: _____

_____

Our family packing style is:
(check one)

○ **The Orderly O'Briens:** We make lists and check them twice! Every bag and suitcase is neatly and properly packed the day before we leave for a trip. We rarely forget things.

○ **The Semi-Structured Smiths:** For the most part, each member of our family is an organized packer. A couple of us are overpackers, and there are always a few things that we forget.

○ **The Messy Mancinis:** If we could stuff the kitchen sink into a suitcase, we would! Our policy is: stuff some clothes in a duffle bag and run. We're not big on planning, but we always seem to bring along what we need (and some things we probably don't need, too!).

Our group overpacker was _____
He/she had the biggest bag of all!

Our group underpacker was _____
His/her bag was tiny!

What we forgot to bring: _____

Music that we brought with us: _____
_____
_____

Games that we packed: _____
_____
_____

Books that we packed: _____
_____
_____

New clothes that we bought for the trip: _____

Before we leave on trips, we always_____

_____

ARE WE THERE YET?!

We traveled by
(check one or more)

O Car

O Boat

O Plane

O Train

O Bus

O Go-Cart

O Bicycle

O Ferry

O Messenger pigeon

Here are our tickets !

Paste your ticket stubs here

28E

0503 28JUL07

AMSTERDAM/AMS

KEFLAVIK

...TURE TIME: 14.00

...RITY NO: 044

Anchorage

Vancouver

Toronto

Chicago

New York

Los Angeles

Dallas

Miami

Mexico City

Bogotá

Cusco

Rio de Janeiro

Santiago

PASSPORT

Our Travel Route

Draw a star over your home location and a star over your vacation location. Then, connect the two stars with a dotted line.

St. Petersburg

London

Paris

Madrid

Rome

Marrakech

Cairo

New Delhi

Shanghai

Tokyo

Hong Kong

Bangkok

Cape Town

Sydney

It took us _____ hours to get to our vacation spot.

Our favorite traveling moments:

1._____

2._____

3._____

OUR HOME AWAY FROM HOME

We stayed at _____

It is a _____
(hotel / rental house / friend's house / relative's house)

Our accommodations were:
(circle one)

Awesome

Very Nice

Fine

Not the best

Guest

Our Favorite Things About Where We Stayed

1. _____

2. _____

3. _____

4. _____

5. _____

Staying at _____

was very _____. We especially

liked when _____ decided

to _____. It was so _____!

If we owned a hotel, it would be named _____.

We think that every hotel should always have

_____.

Here's a picture of where we stayed!

Paste a picture here!

H²O

- NO -
VACANCY

SIGHTSEEING TIME!

On our trip, we saw _____

_____

_____

_____

The best words to describe where we visited are
(check as many as apply)

- ○ Exotic
- ○ Metropolitan
- ○ Rural
- ○ Tropical
- ○ Adventurous

- ○ Fast paced
- ○ Old-fashioned
- ○ Mountainous
- ○ Warm
- ○ Cold

- ○ Sunny
- ○ Rainy
- ○ Busy
- ○ Leisurely

Paste or staple your admission tickets to
museums, theme parks, or shows here!

My favorite sight was...

Name:_____ Favorite Sight:_____

Name:_____ Favorite Sight:_____

Name:_____ Favorite Sight:_____

Name:_____ Favorite Sight:_____

Name:_____ Favorite Sight:_____

Five things that we learned while sightseeing:

1._____

_____

2._____

_____

3._____

_____

4._____

_____

5._____

FOOD, GLORIOUS FOOD!

Our favorite restaurant was_____

There we ate:_____

_____

On road trips, we like to eat: _____

_____

The pickiest eater in our family:_____

The most adventurous eater in our family:

_____

Local Specialties:_____

_____

_____

The worst meal of the trip:_____

_____

The funniest meal of the trip:_____

_____

The weirdest food we tried:_____

_____

STARTERS

SOUPS

Paste a picture here!

NEW PLACES, FRIENDLY FACES
People we visited and met along the way...

Paste a picture here!

Paste a picture here!

CAMERA

Paste a picture here!

SPEAK french

Paste a picture here!

Paste a picture here!

Paste a picture here!

LIBERTY

Say Cheese! Our Family Photos

Paste a picture here!

Paste a picture here!

Paste a picture here!

Paste a picture here!

Paste a picture here!

Paste a picture here!

OUR DREAM VACATION

Abs. 16. Gr. ... ? Verein No 14 über Hannover (20)

If we could go anywhere in the universe, we would visit _____
_____

We would stay for _____

Here's what we would do: _____
_____

Here's how we would get there: _____
_____

We would stay at a _____
_____

MY DREAM VACATION
(because sometimes we have different opinions!)

Name:_____

If I was in charge we would visit:_____

_____

Name:_____

If I was in charge we would visit:_____

_____

Name:_____

If I was in charge we would visit:_____

_____

Name:_____

If I was in charge we would visit:_____

_____

Name:_____

If I was in charge we would visit:_____

_____

MAKING MEMORIES

Our best day: _____

_____

Our funniest vacation moment: _____

_____

Our happiest vacation moment: _____

_____

New things that we learned about each other: _____

_____

The best part about going on vacation: _____

_____

Things that we want to do next time we take a trip: _____

_____

Place a photo here!

BIG BEN

DO NOT DISTURB

NOTICE: Guests who do not wish to be disturbed, hang this card on the outside door-knob.

Goodbye! *Au revoir!*
See you soon!
¡ADIOS! CIAO! AUF
WIEDERSEHEN
SAYONARA!

(Have every member of the family vacation party sign this post-card)

Made in Germany

Post Card

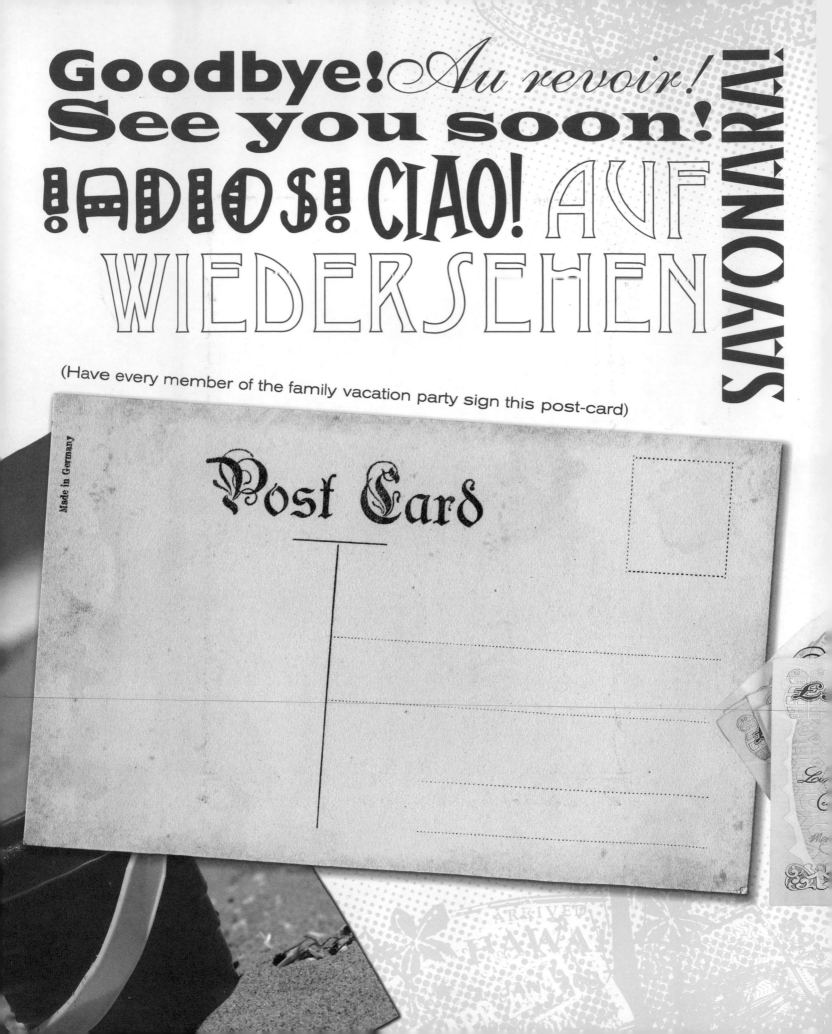